BEN OKRI is the author of 10 novels, including *The Famished Road*, which won the Booker prize, and *The Age of Magic*, as well as volumes of poetry, short stories and essays. His work has been translated into more than 26 languages and has won numerous international prizes. He is a Fellow of the Royal Society of Literature, Vice-President of the English Centre of International PEN, and Patron of the International School of Storytelling. Born in Nigeria, he lives in London.

To Katherine,
A spell is cast that you find your writer's voice. But first write and read a lot.
Stay open —

The Mystery Feast

Thoughts on Storytelling

Ben Okri

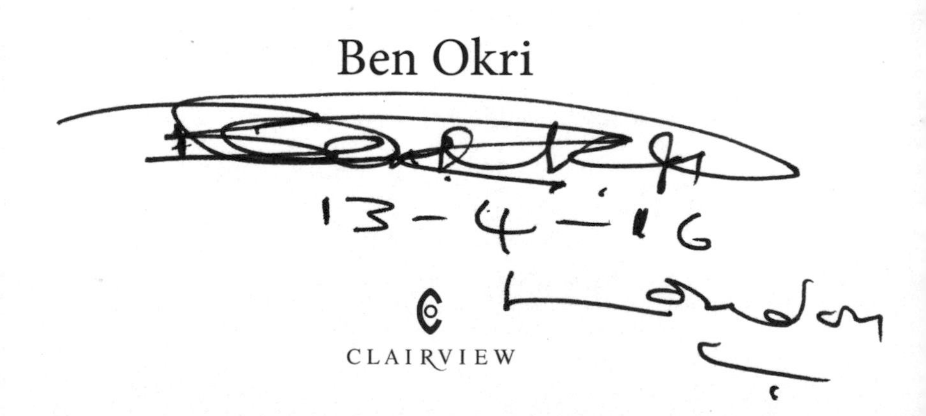

13-4-16
London

CLAIRVIEW

Clairview Books Ltd.,
Russet, Sandy Lane,
West Hoathly,
West Sussex RH18 5ES

www.clairviewbooks.com

Published in Great Britain in 2015 by Clairview Books in association with the
International School of Storytelling, 8 The Drive, Hove, East Sussex BN3 3JF

www.schoolofstorytelling.com

A CIP catalogue record for this book is available from the British Library

Print book ISBN 978 1 905570 76 8
Ebook ISBN 978 1 905570 67 6

Design and typesetting by yellowfishdesign.co.uk
Cover art: 'From the Magic Lamp' by Rosemary Clunie. Author photo by Metsavend
Printed and bound by Gutenberg Press Ltd, Malta

Contents

1. All we do

All we do

Gazing at the shape of a hill,
The grey horizon,
A woman reading a book,
A landscape shaped by history.
All we do is story.

Our public acts are dreams.
Our private acts are dramas.
Submerged rivers are our thoughts,
Misted streams our hopes.

Like the spider we turn
All things into ourselves.
We bend the light
Of time into fables.

Beyond our mind, reality moves.
Unknowable like the darkness
Before creation.

We carve from the unknown
A world.
Without story
Our identities
Starve.

We live in and out
Of time
Simultaneously.

Living belongs to story.
Being belongs to mystery.
Beyond form
Our souls
Breathe.

We yield time
Our story-making sense.
In this portion of eternity,
Awake and in dreams,
We live myths.
It's what makes us immense.

2. Under the Sun

A meditation on stories

Notes to a modern storyteller

Address given at the
"Everything Under the Sun
Storytelling Festival"

Hosted by the
International School of Storytelling
at Emerson College
23 August 2013

One

There is nothing that expresses the roundedness of human beings more than storytelling. Stories are the highest technology of being.

There is in story the greatest psychology of existence, of living. Indeed there is in story something semi-divine. The nature of story itself is linked to the core of creation. Story belongs to the micro-moment after the big bang. It belongs to the micro-moment after the 'let there be light!' act of creation.

We live in a time in which we are being told that the main things of value are the things of science and the things of technology. Our lives are being compressed into this technological reality. But it is worth remembering the many-sidedness of being human. Great evil befalls us when we restrict ourselves to just one side of our being.

It is important that we don't become machines, that we don't become computers. We contain machines. We contain computers. We contain all of nature, the seas, the mountains, the constellations, and the nearly infinite spaces.

At the heart of all science — its experiments, its theories, its mathematics, its discoveries, its interpretations — is the story instinct. The scientific mind would be impossible without the story DNA, without the story-seeing brain cells. The mind's aspects do not operate in isolation. Every human being immersed in the cyclorama of reality is implicated in the cosmic story-making nature of reality. Maybe this story-making quality of reality is what constitutes the heart of our existence.

At every moment we are in a micro or macro 'once upon a time' sea of existence. In every moment we are part of the infinite stories that the universe is telling us, and that we are telling the universe.

Maybe this story-making quality of being is the principle magic as well as the principle illusion of our lives. Maybe what the Buddha is indicating through meditation is transcending this story-making quality of the mind and arriving at the absolute reality that lies behind all things. When this is glimpsed, it is called Nirvana. From this perspective, the storytelling quality of being is temporal. It is a necessary illusion, but the final one which we must transcend.

But then maybe this storytelling quality of mind is itself a paradox and a metaphor of that which we are finally meant to discover. The kiss that awakens the princess from her bed of sleep is not just the kiss of romance but maybe also the kiss of enlightenment. A true awakening is an enlightenment. This is especially so when you consider sleep as the metaphor of our unawakened condition in the true wonder of reality.

Stories are the koans that life sends us. They contain hints of multiple realities.

The great stories, which appear all over the world in different variations, are intuitions sensed about this mysterious nature of the absolute reality. Great stories have lightness and multi-dimensional agility. They speak constantly to different levels in us. They speak to us at the level that we are on.

The story about the seven dwarves can be a coded reference to class conditions in society. It could also be the imagination's grasp of fundamental patterns at work in the cellular dimension of our bodies. It could be a metaphysical understanding of the mystery of numbers. The story is never really just about seven dwarves, or it would not linger in the imagination.

We treat stories like dustbins into which we dispose our lowest sense of possibilities. The tale of the Emperor's

New Clothes is alluded to whenever we talk about something that is less than it appears to be. That same story can be just as much about the power of true seeing. In a world of advertisements, obsession with fame, in which the hyped is more valued than the true, the tale of the Emperor's New Clothes gains significant resonance. Most of what we pursue, what we are obsessed with, what confuses and humiliates us, most of what society projects at us, the inflated notions of success, are all Emperor's New Clothes. We have bought into the way of seeing that believes all the illusions are actually the velvet royal cloak, richly to be desired. We need to be that little boy who can see most of the stuff of society as exactly what it is — mass projection and emptiness.

One story read the right way can turn our false world upside down and restore to us a true sense of sanity. For the world drives us mad with its foolishness. It has been doing this for centuries. We have slowly become aware of it and have distilled our awareness. We have planted that distillation in the most memorable and indestructible place we can find. We have made that place a constant guide to ourselves in our endless incarnations. The place in which we plant them are stories.

Stories are the infinite seeds that we have brought with us through the millennia of walking the dust of the earth. They are our celestial pods. They are our alchemical cauldrons. If we listen to them right, if we read them deeply, they will guide us through the confusion of our lives, and the diffusion of our times.

Stories are never what they seem. They are whispers from beyond the invisible screen of existence. They are whisperings from the gods we carry within us.

Two

Stories bear the same relation to us that dreams do. Except that stories are coherent dreaming. Where do we think that stories come from anyway? Do we think we entirely make them up? Do we think that Homer wholly invented *The Odyssey*? Or that a single human being imagined *The Tales of One Thousand and One Nights*? Or that Shakespeare originated *The Tempest*? There is a presumption in thinking that we entirely invent our stories. Rather it could be said that the stories come through us, assemble themselves out of the elements of our lives and imagination. We receive and shape them. We cannot be said to originate them. All true storytellers are modest.

This also hints at the true value of stories. Why do we tell them? Why should we pay attention to them? It may be because they come from beyond, from some uncommon living, ever-evolving, universal storehouse of wisdom.

Stories appear to bend themselves to our time. That may be because, in order to exist, stories must intersect with time. The difficulties human beings face, the enigmas of life, will not go away. They will not go away till we are perfected. And we are not going to be perfected for a very long time.

Therefore to read a true story, or to listen to one, is not to experience the story of the person who wrote it, or the person who tells it. It is to read or listen to the genius of the tribe and the race. It is to listen to the genius of humanity.

They are not given to us merely to read or listen to. They are also given to us to amplify, interpret, and to live. All good stories are practical guides for living, or negative guides on how not to live. Maybe our contemporary ethos is unwise in over-emphasising the technological aspects of modern society. One of the most invaluable qualities to also develop in a people is imagination. We tend to emphasise knowledge over imagination. It is as important to know how to acquire facts as it is to understand how the world works. But knowledge is empty without imagination, without spirit, without the heart.

No civilisation ever became great on knowledge alone.

Indeed it is the imaginative dimension of civilisations which gives them distinction. What would ancient Greece be without its tragedians, its Parthenon, its Homeric epics? What would ancient Egypt be without its pyramids, its temples? Imagination dreams that which knowledge makes real. It could be said that imagination is the proto-reality. A people can only create what they can imagine. If in some mysterious way we fall short of the ancients, it may be because we have long ceased to cultivate, to the highest degree, the fruits of the imagination, of the spirit. That despairing cry from the bible should always haunt us. 'For lack of vision my people perish.'

How do we awaken imagination? How do we awaken vision? One of the ways, passed down to us with cunning simplicity by our ancestors, is storytelling. But it takes many forms. A painting on a cave wall of a man pursuing a bison is a story. The frescoes of Giotto in Assisi are distilled stories. Stories are intersections between mortality and immortality. When we tell stories some immortal part of ourselves is singing in time. When we tell stories the ages awaken. When we listen to stories our future takes clearer shape. That which is beyond time is wiser than time. Somewhere I wrote that stories can conquer fear. That is because fear comes from unknowing, and stories help us know a little more. The things the heart knows shine a greater light than the things the head knows.

Take the story of *The Odyssey*, and the twenty-year adventure of trying to get home. It tells us a hundred things, and each moment of the story tells us a hundred more. Why did Odysseus answer 'Nobody' when Polyphemus asked him his name? On one level it is a cunning ruse. On another, interpretative level, it hints perhaps that we are someone specific and no one. In being nobody he could be everybody.

What does the story of Penelope mean? Every night she undoes the weaving she did during the day. On one level it is a cunning act of delay, worthy of the wife of Odysseus. On another interpretative level, we sense that this is what life does, what sleep does every night, what death does at the end of every life.

Take the story of *Cinderella*. She is the one who is ignored, who does the hard work of cleaning, while the two elder sisters get to go to the ball. Yet it is her foot the slipper fits. On one level this is a tale of wish fulfilment. On another level it could be seen as a hint of the rewards of humility. It could also be seen as a parable about those who might inherit the earth, that it is not the showy ones, the evidently beautiful ones, or the famous ones that the true riches of the kingdom come to, but perhaps those who toil unseen.

Have you noticed that when someone does something astounding, publishes an important new novel, makes an invaluable new scientific discovery, or creates an amazing new work of art, the press always says 'they came from nowhere'? They didn't come from nowhere. They came from where Cinderella came from, toiling in the unglamorous back rooms of their chosen field, wherever life has led them.

The idea that most girls have, that they are Cinderella, and will gain Cinderella's crown, is to miss acres of its possible interpretations. The truth is that because of her hard work, her obedience, her humility, her goodness of spirit, her kindliness, her toughness, her quiet initiative, because of all these things and more, which the tale only hints at, Cinderella is the most deserving of the sisters. She earned her glory by her toil and her spirit, and not by the appropriate size of her feet. In this story her feet are merely the symbol of having walked the right path.

Three

Great stories are wiser than we are. They are enigmas. We never get to the bottom of them anymore than we get to the bottom of ourselves. Great stories are furled universes. They are like computer programmes that contain within them an infinity of secret programmes.

To enter into the world of a good story is to leave the horizontal limitation of reality behind. In the world of great stories all is verticality and diagonality. The inner world of stories operates according to the laws of spirals and loops. In ordinary reality events appear sequential, linked by everyday logic. In the world of good stories everything is linked by surprise. There only the unpredictable is logical. The laws of the world of stories operate inversely to those of the world we call reality.

As this is a celebration of storytelling, it is also important to state that stories can also be pernicious. Stories have also been used for evil. They have been used for the denigration, the demonisation, and the extermination of peoples. This is because of the psychological power of stories, their ability to fit in perfectly with our belief brain cells. It is easier to get people to believe nasty things about others if you tell nasty stories about them.

Stories, used as negative propaganda, have fuelled

wars, tribal dissensions, and genocide. False stories use the same laws as good stories, making them readily acceptable to our imagination. The true danger of stories is that they tend to bypass reason. They can bypass intelligence and go straight to the subconscious. Why else have very intelligent people in the past believed such absurd things about other races? The subliminal demonisation in stories and images is one of the roots of racism and sexism. All kinds of outsiders suffer also from this cruel misuse of mental association that stories can promote.

When they want to destroy a people they begin telling stories about them. Even when negative stories about a people are not believed they still leave an imprint on the underside of the mind, a residuum of doubt, a sinister grain that in time can become an evil pus of perception. Then one day, with the insistent provocation by demagogues, a people might rise up and slaughter those who have been demonised by stories, 'the other'. The ancient Greeks did it with the Persians. The Romans with stories built Carthage into a monstrous foe which must be exterminated, and this culminated in their destruction. They did it with the Africans during the slave trade, the Jews before the Holocaust, they did it with the Tutsis, they did it with black South Africans during Apartheid, and they are doing it now to one group of people or another, and they do it through rumours in the media and with our passive collusion.

Whenever we listen to negative stories about others we are contributing to this ongoing preparation for some unforeseen future monstrosity. Tyrants and ideologues use stories; the state uses stories when it wants to bend our inclination towards its secret programmes. The cold war was a time of the toxicity of stories. Families use them to create their own myths, sometimes at the expense of other branches of the family. People use stories about their friends. Stories are dangerous because they can be easily misused. The Grimm brothers made stepmothers figures of eternal suspicion. But in the original stories the Grimm brothers drew from, the people who did those terrible deeds were not the stepmothers, but the mothers. The Brothers Grimm, rewriting those stories, felt they could not allow mothers to be so traduced. So they traduced stepmothers instead.

Stories are not innocent. We should be careful about the stories we listen to. We should be sceptical and critical. We should always ask questions about them and seek to make a distinction in our minds between good and false stories.

The law of stories is immortal. Stories invariably reveal their secret truth. False stories in the end tend us towards evil, towards injustice, towards unfairness. Good stories tend us towards clarity and transcendence.

Four

Good stories incline towards life, towards the raising of consciousness, a lifting of the heart. They are evolutionary. For good stories point the way upwards. This is their enigma. It is not enough to read or listen to them. We must continually meditate on them to extract their timeless wisdom, their signposts meant to guide us on the true secret path.

We should never forget that stories have a hidden life, a sleeping potential. Only a significant experience or constant meditation wakes us up to their many mansions of truth.

We speak of life in society and in communities, we speak of politics and government, but there is finally only one life—stories are holistic because they address all aspects of this one life.

Storytellers, reclaim your power to shape the future through stories. You are descendants of the bards and the wonder-workers. Only in recent centuries have storytellers become divorced from the power of making, the power of affecting reality.

In ancient Africa, in Celtic lands, storytellers were magicians. They were initiates. They understood the underlying nature of reality, its hidden forces. The old Celtic bards could bring out welts on the body with a string of syllables. They could heal sickness with a tale. They could breathe life into a dying civilisation with the magic of a story. To a thriving civilisation, they could bring transformation with the potency of a myth. In the old days kings and leaders, warriors and knights listened to epic tales and drew from them courage and inspiration.

The historian deals with the past, but the true storyteller works with the future. You can tell the strength of an age by the imaginative truth-grasping vigour of its storytellers. Stories are matrices of thought. They are patterns formed in the mind. They weave their effect on the future. To be a storyteller is to work with, to weave with, the material of time itself.

A nation is shaped by the stories its children are told. A nation is sustained by the stories it tells itself. The good stories can liberate its potential, or help it face the dragons of its evils.

Storytellers, reclaim the fire and sorcery of your estate. Take an interest in everything. You cannot be a magician in stories if you are not a magician in life. Go forward into the future, but also return to the great secret gnosis of the bards.

As the world gets more confused, storytellers should become more centred. What we need in our age are not more specialists, experts, spin-doctors. What we need are people deeply rooted in the traditions of their art, but who are also at ease in the contemporary world.

We need storytellers who weave their tales with far-seeing eyes, and multi-dimensional hearts. We need storytellers who know something. Not those who dabble, who turn out words merely for pay or for fame.

Storytellers are the singing conscience of the land, the unacknowledged guides.

Reclaim your power to help our age become wise again. Help us find our way, that we may travel that great road that fell into ruin when we abandoned the mysteries.

Notes to a modern storyteller

1

The most sensational stories are not necessarily the ones that endure.

2

The stories that last are the ones most cunningly, most mysteriously, told.

3

The greatness of a story is more in the telling than in the tale. The true art resides in the nature of the telling, the way the story is freighted to the imagination. There are more sensational stories than the Odyssey, but few as enigmatically told.

4

Our age is lost in sensational tales. Without genuine mystery, the mystery of art, a story will not linger in the imagination.

5

A fragment is more fascinating than the whole.

6

The mind likes completion. If you give the mind complete stories you give it nothing to do. The Trojan war lasted twenty years. But Homer tells only of one year, one quarrel, one rage. Yet has a war haunted us more? It is the war story to which others return, as to a source.

7

Indirection fascinates. Straight roads make the mind fall asleep. But we all love to take hidden paths, roads that bend and curve. The Renaissance artists understood the appeal of paths that wander out of view. We want to travel the untravelled road. We should learn to tell untold stories; stories that wander off the high road; stories like roads untaken.

This is the only cure for the despair that all the stories have been told, that there are no new stories under the sun. All the high road stories have been told, but not the hidden roads stories that lead to the true centre.

8

Direct things bore us. Indirect things awaken us. Indirection wakens us to the wonder of the world. Poetry is restored to the world through suggestiveness. Indirect stories stimulate the imagination. Indirect writing multiplies reality.

9

The way a story is told affects the reality of the story. A story is altered by its telling, its slant, its accent, its angle. The mode of telling is a portal. A new portal makes a new story.

10

A story exists in language, but lives in the imagination, in the memory. When does a story live? It lives only when it is read or heard. A story is part telling, part hearing. Part writing, part reading. It dwells in the ambiguous place between the teller and the hearer, between the writer and the reader. The greatest storytellers understand this magical fact, and use the magic of the in-between in their stories and in their telling.

11

A story is a spirit essence. It wanders the ether till an open heart, a receptive mind, gives it habitation.

12

A story is not a thing. It is a perpetual potentiality. An endlessly coiled energy. It sleeps in its Elysium till it is brought into the realm of human beings.

13

Stories are the purest form of self revealing. Every story you write or tell reveals you. It is impossible to conceal yourself in your stories. More revealing than the face, are the stories you tell. A story is the most self-betraying act we engage in.

We are never more naked than in our stories.

The time will come when we will be able to predict how long a person will live, their health, their success or failure in life, from the stories they write or tell. Just as every cell in our body carries the genetic make-up of the whole entity, so every story carries within it the encoded fate, future, and possibilities of its tellers, its writers, its singers.

14

Maybe the life of a nation — its health, its spiritual strength — can be deduced from the stories the nation tells, the stories it suppresses, the stories it sanctions.

But this self-betraying aspect of story functions in a shadow way. Nations that tell themselves stories of how great they are may suffer from a pathology. The stories told may be truly revelatory not in the stories themselves, but in the shadows cast, in the dark national deeds, in the nation's undiagnosed neurosis.

15

We incubate stories like maggots in rotting meat. We incubate stories like spores.

16

Our secret stories, operating in the depths of our psyches, are the true determinants of our lives. The most potent stories are not the public stories we tell about ourselves. The most potent stories are secret stories in our psyches, in our deeper selves. We have no obvious control over these stories. It is these secret stories, these underground, underworld stories that a nation tells itself, that an individual tells itself, in the night, while it sleeps. It is these stories that truly shape our lives. It is these stories which must be changed if destinies are to change.

3. The story in the next room

A Stoku

The story in the next room

A group of us were in the big room. Next door, in the small room, there was a young lady. She had been by herself for a long time.

'Why don't we ask her to come and tell us a story?' someone said.

'Why would she want to tell a story?' I said.

'Just ask her.'

'Why should I ask her?'

'Go on.'

So I went next door and knocked. I thought I heard her say come in. I went in and saw her sitting on the bed. She was young and fair-skinned and had full fluffy hair. For a moment I found it hard to speak. She looked me and said nothing. I said:

'Would you come next door and tell us a story?'

'Why?'

'Why not?'

I knew why not. She was shy. She had that shyness of youth. It was a shyness that was also an affectation.

'Come on,' I said. 'What would it cost you?'

'I can't.'

'Why not?'

'You know why not.'

'Come on.'

I saw it now as a challenge. I didn't need to. They had asked me to ask her, and now I wanted to see if I could get her to do it. I pleaded with her. She wouldn't budge.

I became aware they were watching us through the little pane of glass. I could see their faces crowded into the square pane, watching to see if I would succeed.

She kept looking at me. I could see that her shyness wouldn't let her do it, but I kept asking her anyway. At last she said:

'I won't come and tell a story, but I'll do this.'

Then she took off her top. I tried not to look. They were fresh and small.

'Come next door and tell us a story. We'd like that.

What would a story cost you anyway?'

'I just can't,' she said.

She regarded me with grey-blue eyes. The faces were still pressed close to the semi-frosted glass. I pleaded with her once more, but she was looking down at the black top in her lap.

'I wish I could, but I can't,' she said, still looking down.

Maybe I shouldn't go on pleading with her, I thought. She doesn't want to tell a story. It's not easy telling a story. Most people would do anything than tell a story. Maybe I should leave her alone.

But now she was staring at me. It seemed like a challenge. I didn't move, but nor did she.

'Why don't you tell me a story,' she said.

'Me?'

'Yes.'

She gestured to the faces pressed to the glass, and they all came in. They sat on the bed.

'He's going to tell us a story,' she said.

I hadn't noticed when she put her top back on. They were all looking at me. It was quite frightening. They looked as if they were going to devour me. In order to stop them I had to tell a story. I took a deep breath, and began.

'One day,' I said, ' I walked out through my front door, and saw a Tiger...'

Little Venice,
London.

The International School of Storytelling is the longest running centre of its kind where the craft of the storyteller is practiced and honoured. Here stories come alive and serve performers, healers, teachers, activists, environmentalists and the wider community. Whether an experienced teller or a beginner to the art, everyone is welcome here.

www.schoolofstorytelling.com

The School was established in 1994. In 2011 it became an independent Charity and continues to be based at Emerson College, East Sussex, although its work takes place all over the world.

International School of Storytelling Limited
Registered in England and Wales no. 7506833. Registered Charity no. 1143285